"I believe there are three very important relationships in life, and they are all represented at the Cross of Jesus: Relationship with God, with others and with ourselves. This latter relationship with ourselves is probably the one least explored in our church circles.

Adriana has been able to present to us an easy read seven-day manual to improve our understanding of ourselves. Each chapter comes with a very personal story that helps bring home the principle Adriana is presenting and makes it easy to implement the application at the end of the chapter. I highly recommend you read this manual over seven days and meditate on each day's probing questions and action points and you will increase in your everyday effectiveness and understanding of how and for what purpose you were created."

PASTOR RAUL BURGOS
COMUNIDAD CRISTIANA, Elizabeth, NJ

"Adriana has been a good friend for many years, she has inspired me and everyone around her. I can truly say that her heart was poured out into this project and I believe that this book will help you and guide you to start seeing yourself as God created you to be: "His masterpiece"!

PASTOR JUCELIO DA SILVA
HOME INTERNATIONAL CHURCH, Kearny, NJ

"Adriana's book is such a powerfully effective strategy guide for life. With real life testimonies, biblical principles, and insightful breakdowns of truth that will surely both challenge and inspire the way you think and feel. A must have guide out of the dark into the light."

DEBORA UGALDE
PASTOR, AUTHOR OF "Quiero ser Feliz", California.

When you read this book, you will taste and see that the Lord is good and He wants us to be better than just "good." Blessed is the man who takes refuge in Him. Psalm 34:8. Once you have tasted it, you will know how sweet your life is to be. You will discover a deeper purpose step by step. Joy will come upon you like a flood. Peace will penetrate your heart and not leave you. A whole new life awaits you. The power within you will be unleashed. You will walk on fire, and not get burned. I have been blessed to walk with Pastor Adriana for 12 years, and this book is an application of her personal experiences that were given to her specifically to be used to help us transform our lives and bring us to a point of no return. Romans 12:2. Don't copy the behavior and customs of this world, but let God transform you into a new person by changing the way you think. Then you will learn to know God's will for you, which is good and pleasing and perfect. Let Pastor Adriana lead you to Him and let Him transform you to a wholesome discovered new you. What are you waiting for?
Friends to eternity...Love you my friend.

ELISA AMBROSIO-FARIAS, Esq.
Newark NJ

A SEVEN DAY DEVOTIONAL

FIND YOURSELF FIRST

REINVENTING LIFE FROM THE INSIDE

ADRIANA FERREIRA
CERTIFIED LIFE COACH

FIND YOURSELF FIRST by Adriana Ferreira

Published by God's Life Publishing

NEW JERSEY
742 Chancellor Avenue
Irvington, NJ 07111

HAWAII
4998C E. Ehiku Way
Ewa Beach, HI 96706

Email: godlife@aol.com   www.godslifepublishing.org

This book or parts thereof may not be reproduced in any form, stored in a retrieval system, or transmitted in any form by any means—electronic, mechanical, photocopy, recording, or otherwise for commercial gain or profit—without prior written permission of the publisher. The use of short quotations or occasional page copying for personal or group study is permitted and encouraged.

Unless otherwise identified, Scripture quotations are from the King James Version of the Bible.

Designed by God's Life Publishing

Copyright ©2018 by Adriana Ferreira
All rights reserved

International Standard Book Number: 978-0-9916263-8-0

Printed in the United States of America

I WOULD LIKE TO
DEDICATE THIS BOOK
TO

MY FIRST LOVE,

MY LORD

AND

MY SAVIOR

JESUS CHRIST

FIND YOURSELF FIRST

SPECIAL THANKS

Special thanks to my incredible husband Eddie and my kids Kevin and Kathlyn who bring so much joy into my life. To Bishop Calvin and his wife Dr. Melrose Bethea who believed in my work and made a dream come true. And to all of my friends, family and church community who have always supported, helped and shaped me.

I am forever grateful for being surrounded by such remarkable people.

**Iron sharpeneth iron;
so a man sharpeneth
the countenance of his friend.
Proverbs 27:17**

FIND YOURSELF FIRST

TABLE OF CONTENTS

Foreword 11

Introduction 13

Day 1: *You Are The Missing Piece* 23
Facing Comparison 25

Day 2: *You Are God's Perfect Design* 31
Facing Unforgiveness 35

Day 3: *You Are More Than Enough* 39
Facing Regret 41

Day 4: *You Are Strong* 45
Facing Fear 48

Day 5: *You Are Flawless* 53
Facing Pride 56

Day 6: *You Are An Inspiration* 61
Facing Low Self-Esteem 64

Day 7: *You Are Unlimited* 69
Facing Procrastination 72

About the Author 77

Contact The Author 79

FIND YOURSELF FIRST

FOREWORD

Have you ever felt like resetting your life and starting all over again? Have you ever thought how amazing it would be if we could suddenly push a button and start living another reality? Well although it is not so simple, like pushing a button, we are also not destined to live trapped in harmful and hurtful emotions for the rest of our lives; there is an exit.

In this book you will find some principles that will challenge you to look in the mirror and have an encounter with yourself that will propel you out of the comfort zone and victimhood to take on the unique genuine identity that God has given you.

Adriana is part of my team. I have had the privilege of walking close to her and her family for almost two decades and it has been rewarding to see her growth personally, professionally and as a pastor. I have witnessed the success of applying the principles she deals with in this book, and certainly this will not be different with you.

In Christ we have the opportunity to be born again and to enjoy a new and joyful life.

When God created us he had a work of art in his mind, and however much the world and life might damage and destroy us, in Christ we can begin all over again and reconnect with His original design.

My sincere wish is that God will bless you during this reading and transform you, so that you can be all that he has created you to be.

> *"Therefore, if any man be in Christ, he is a new creature: old things are passed away; behold, all things have become new.*
> 2 Corinthians 5:17

Marcelo De Souza Senior Pastor
Home International Church, Kearny, NJ

INTRODUCTION

For what is a man profited, if he shall gain the whole world, and lose his own soul? or what shall a man give in exchange for his soul?
Matthew 16:26

Every day that we wake into, we are presented with a new opportunity to discover, conquer, and to enjoy the life we were given freely by God. How do you start your day? Some people will have a morning tea or a glass of water, or they'll just take a nice shower to cool off to start the day rolling.

Do you start worrying about the traffic?

Do you stress over the clothes you'll have to wear?

Do you get anxious about school projects and presentations?

Do you feel frustrated with that pile of dirty laundry you must take care of?

Or do you let the thoughts of failure and regret slow you down?

With so much on our plate, mornings can be overwhelming and frustrating if we fail to give it life.

Every day, we wake up knowing that there is a world out there, and we have a very big chance to get out and conquer, win our battle, and achieve that goal if we put to work; we want to nail that interview, get our laundry done, present that project, fix a closet, or make that appointment, but many times, we don't even know where to start. And then right when we are about to take some action, creepy feelings visit our heart and make us doubt our readiness.

Thoughts of discouragement enter our minds and predispose us to second-guess it or even give up.

How many times have you heard the voices of procrastination, fear, and rejection stopping you from exploring and enjoying your daily activities? How many times did those voices make you compare yourself to others and question if you would ever be good enough?

We look for things to fulfill us, to give us answers, to motivate us, but hardly do we take some time to let God speaks to us so as to activate the answers or solutions we long for.

We tend to listen to our emotions or what I simply call "the voice of the enemy"— which constantly tells us that we can't, it's too hard, and it's not for us, and most of the time, we don't even question them or even make an attempt to fight the ill thoughts.

We surround ourselves with information trying to

explain our behavior or lack of it and find names for our conditions without really taking some time to question and evaluate where the voices are coming from and, most importantly, whether those voices are really true. And even if they are and they remind you of your past failures, should they define who you are now?

I used to believe that those voices were true. Thoughts of pessimism used to play in my mind, reminding me of my past mistakes and situations that hurt me. They would constantly discourage me from taking any bold step. They always left me feeling like there was something missing in my life.

I was always looking for it. I tried looking for it in knowledge, in friendship, in marriage, in a successful career, and even in motherhood. All of it helped tremendously. It was part of the process. But it was through a closer relationship with Jesus that I found the missing piece of this puzzle called "life." As I learned to set aside some time to experience the peace that flows from God's presence, it helped me to trust Him no matter what my circumstances are.

Silence and stillness have many proven benefits. Besides, replenishing our mental resources and regenerating the brain cells, it boosts our mood, makes us aware of our surroundings, and makes us more sensitive to God's presence in our lives.

I discovered that true happiness is available, but it only comes from within, and it is not attached to circumstances. When we take time to be alone, to disconnect from our surroundings, we would experience the presence of God, and the strength that only comes from Him rescues us and takes us to *our* base: the essence of our soul.

I have learned that as we get closer to God, those voices begins to work in our favor if we look at them as an opportunity for a breakthrough. This reminds me of the story in the Bible about David and Goliath.

The people of Israel were being oppressed by the continuous threat of Goliath. The giant would come forward every morning and evening for forty days, intimidating the Israelites until a young man named David decided to do something different about it. He faced the giant using what he had—a sling and a stone—and defeated Goliath because he believed that God's favor was upon him. He wasn't a strong man physically, but he knew how to use his resources and allowed God to do His part. Defeating Goliath was one of David's greatest accomplishments, which resulted to his fame as a brave warrior. David became a champion in the fight because of his great trust in God's power. Goliath was David's breakthrough.

Ignoring the voices of the enemy is not the answer, but activating that bravery and confronting them with the truth found in the Word of God will set you free through the power of Christ, who lives inside of those who believe in Him.

> *...because greater is he that is in*
> *you, than he that is in the world.*
>
> 1 John 4:4b

I want to challenge you to embark on a very simple journey to *find yourself first* by taking some time to get to know yourself through God's lenses, and enjoy who God made you to be. When we allow His love to fulfill us, it will set us free from the limited perception about ourselves. Sometimes, you just need to accept that you made a mistake, that you were hurt by somebody, or that you need help so that you can deal with it and move on.

This book is a simple daily resource to help you organize your thoughts and coach your emotions daily. Each day, you'll have a different approach and goal in life. I would encourage you to take a few minutes apart for yourself daily so that you can read it, reflect on what you read, close your eyes, breathe, and let God do the work inside of you while you rest in His unfailing love that knows no bounds.

As you enjoy your alone time, start by giving thanks to Him, then express your feelings and worries, and let silence take over. As you breathe, just let go of whatever burden you bear, and let stillness take control. You might feel the need to ask for forgiveness, to let go of anger, or to experience peace.

It is in the stillness that our mind stops reasoning, our heart stops sorrowing, and our spirit is revived.

> *"Come unto me, all you who labor and are heavy laden, and I will give you rest."*
>
> Matthew 11:28

Cause me to hear

thy lovingkindness in the morning;

for in thee do I trust: cause me to know

the way wherein I should walk;

for I lift up my soul unto thee.

Deliver me, O Lord, from mine enemies:

I flee unto thee to hide me.

Teach me to do thy will; for thou art my God:

thy spirit is good; lead me into the land of uprightness.

Quicken me, O Lord, for thy name's sake: for thy righteousness' sake bring my soul out of trouble.

And of thy mercy cut off mine enemies,

and destroy all them that afflict my soul:

for I am thy servant.

Psalms 143:8-12

Day 1:

YOU ARE THE MISSING PIECE

"Plagiarism is illegal, so be your own original copy."

Accepting your personality can sometimes be hard to do, especially if you were constantly criticized in the past, made a few bad decisions over delicate issues, or were a victim of bullies like me. My teenage years left me thinking that I would never be good enough and that I needed to be someone else to be happy. The environment and situation I had to face brought about a low self-esteem that affected my growth as a teenager. I was hidden in this thought of pessimism.

Many people grew up comparing themselves to others and developed some sort of inferiority complex within their mental state, and this has caused them to live their lives by other people's standards instead of striving to rediscover their purpose. When you compare yourself, you grossly lose your identity! You are unique. So, when you start feeling condemned by someone's achievements or prideful by someone's lack of merits, it damages you internally and imposes a negative impact in your overall life.

FACING COMPARISON

Why do we always think that the grass is greener on the other side? Have you ever considered that as a good Father, God wholesomely compensates us? Seasons change, and the spring will always be around the corner for those who had a rough season. Sometimes, we are so lost in admiring someone else's land that we forget to enjoy the beauty of our own season placed before us. Whatever success they have achieved awaits us if only we look beyond what we see and be the motivation we desire to effect a change.

> *To everything there is a season, and a time to every purpose under the heaven...*
> Ecclesiastes 3:1

"Never make a permanent decision to a temporary situation."

Today, you might be going through some hardship, but that shouldn't rob you from expecting a change.

When you lack the expectation for a change, you open your heart for resentment to creep and impose negativity on you.

The greatest disadvantage of comparing ourselves is that oftentimes, we get so distracted looking around at what has been built over the years, and end up missing our own target, thereby limiting our dreams and lives. We need to start aiming at our own dreams and work toward achieving them. We all have a duty to be responsible for ourselves in any area of life.

Accept who you are without comparison, without judgment, and without condemnation, and most importantly, do not blame anybody for whatever circumstance that may come your way. Hold yourself responsible for every decision and step you've taken in life's course. Then, and only then, will it become easier to see how amazing you *really* are. Your life will start to change the moment you take full ownership of your problems, decisions, and dreams because you have made yourself the architect of your own fate. Once this has been achieved, you will be adorned with the new opportunities that will lead you to a new you.

When people lack the courage to face their issues in their life, they usually find a way out by blaming others for their misfortunes. Blaming others on your inabilities is acting cowardly because you've lacked the courage to face your fears. When we open our hearts to God and embrace His love, His grace leads us to repentance and a change of attitude. It empowers us to accept our past and present mistakes without condemnation, and it sets us free from our heavy burdens and gives us internal peace and rest.

> *Come unto me, all ye that labour and are heavy laden, and I will give you rest. Take my yoke upon you, and learn of me; for I am meek and lowly in heart: and ye shall find rest unto your souls. For my yoke is easy, and my burden is light.*
>
> Matthew 11:28-30

When I came to the understanding that life wasn't all about what I did but what Jesus did on the cross for me, I discovered that there will always be plenty of time to be happy and living a fulfilled life.

GOD DOES NOT WEAR A WATCH

We need to learn to value ourselves first and trust in our abilities before others can, because sometimes, we expect others to value us when we haven't taken the time to value ourselves. Today, I want you to know that you are the most precious gift to yourself. Your talent is unequaled, your personality is unique, and your loving heart is incomparable.

Because you are His child and He is your Father,

let His unconditional love fill your soul. He knows everything about you and still chases after you. He wants to strengthen your soul and renew your mind daily in His presence.

> **But as many as received him, to them gave the power to become the sons of God.**
> **John 1:12**

As you receive His love and learn to trust in Him, I pray that you will learn to love and respect yourself, to accept who you truly are, to set boundaries, to humble yourself, and to focus on what is important as you embark on life's journey with God.

You are unique because you were created by Him—the great Author and finisher of your faith.

Don't give up. You were lost, but now, you are found in Christ Jesus who strengthens you.

> **...*for this brother was dead, and is alive again; he was lost, and is found."***
> **Luke 15:32b**

❊ How do you see yourself?

❊ What are your unique talents

❊ What kind of pain is keeping you from moving on?

ACCEPT YOURSELF,
TAKE OWNERSHIP OF
YOUR MISTAKES,
AND START LOOKING AT
YOURSELF AS GOD'S
MASTERPIECE.

*For we are his workmanship (*masterpiece*),
created in Christ Jesus unto good works,
which God hath before ordained
that we should walk in them.
Ephesians 2:10*

Day 2:

YOU ARE GOD'S PERFECT DESIGN

Life is like a construction site: always full of choices, decisions, responsibilities, and "oh, what a mess."

When my husband and I were about to execute our long-planned kitchen project, I freaked out at his plans toward it. The plan was to demolish our old kitchen and extend the whole structure of our home toward the backyard. We knew it was going to be very challenging. I remember praying to God, saying, "Please, Lord, don't let me go through this. Make a rich man appear out of nowhere and offer to buy my house for an amazing price so that I can buy a home that already has a brand-new kitchen." I wasn't really motivated to go through the construction process because I knew it was going to be hectic, and this will invariably tell on me due to the tedious nature of the reconstruction process. To be honest, I just wanted to enjoy the results. I wanted a new kitchen without the discomfort of the mess. I just didn't want to undergo any stress. Have you ever asked God to give you a break?

Unfortunately, most of us are guilty of this crime because we ignore the beauty in the mess, fail to recognize the opportunity that lies in the midst of chaos, and that creation is the act of bringing something new into existence!

The Bible tells us that the earth was without form and void and that the Spirit of the Lord was over it. However, when God started to speak His words, creation took place immediately, and the whole mess became an amazing project.

You are not a mistake, and God did not take a break on your life. He already designed you to be more than a conqueror, and He already spoke words of life over you. Stop looking for instant gratification and become passionate about your life and your future.

When we get distracted, we neglect what is important and focus on things that don't count. I was so focused on the mess that I saw as a burden and neglected to work on the design. When the time came to actually pick the colors and the style of my new kitchen cabinets, I wasn't ready to make those decisions, and so I delayed everything.

What I learned is that when you are in the process of building, you don't need to have it all together to bring about a change, but you need to focus on the plan and be responsible for the design because that is what will determine the outcome in the end.

Otherwise, you will end up making the wrong decisions or neglecting what is important. Planning is the most important part of living by faith.

God has planned a great life for each one of us. If we focus on what He has already designed for us, we will most likely make better choices and avoid unnecessary delays that can cause frustrations.

So, be passionate about your own life and grateful to the One who planned, designed, and created you. You have your own story to tell.

Don't downgrade your existence to an evolution experience. That would be totally unfair to your own talents and beauty. A person like you can never be the result of a gradual development but an accomplishment of a single masterpiece by the greatest Artist. You were created, not innovated.

> *"For You formed my inward parts;*
> *You covered me in my mother's womb. I will praise You, for I am fearfully and wonderfully made; Marvelous are Your works,*
> *And that my soul knows very well. My frame was not hidden from You, When I was made in secret, And skillfully wrought in the lowest parts of the earth. Your eyes saw my substance, being yet unformed. And in Your book they all were written, The days fashioned for me,*
> *When as yet there were none of them."*
> Psalms 139:13-16

FACING UNFORGIVENESS

Because people have hurt us in the past, we tend to become limited by the thoughts associated with the pain. Those thoughts passively invades our emotions, causing a mess in the grounds of our hearts just like a messy construction site.

That's when we start keeping track of what went wrong instead of focusing on what has already been accomplished and move on to a better level. Keeping a list of "people to avoid" can really put us in the corner, a cold area where we can't see the possibilities of becoming better, which predisposes us to an unending pain.

When we don't forgive, we become slaves to that pain, and we remain our own prisoner dwelling on a spot. It is a feeling that follows you around while shopping, cooking, and even reading. Our mind plays tricks on us and gets us to think about that person all day long. Forgiveness is an act of kindness toward ourselves. When you forgive, you allow yourself to be free.

Today, I want to encourage you to take a closer look at your list of people you've been avoiding. Examine each situation that brought you pain and consider that each person has a different perspective on life and so they must be forgiven. Remember that we all process things differently and what hurts some might not be that bad for others. Some people will say things impulsively but unintentionally. And even if you still have all the right to prosecute someone, the Bible says that when we judge people, we end up condemning ourselves because we all commit our own sins at some point, yet He forgives us.

We can't change people's perception, but with a good attitude, we can help a person acknowledge that their perception is simply not accurate, which will help them in redirecting their thoughts positively.

We cannot keep people on our list when God Himself sent His only Son to take the place of the list of sinners. It was finished at the cross!

It is time to release the list and let go of the traces of hate in your heart. Let go of those barriers as you take some time to let God revive your soul and set you free.

- How would you define tolerance?
- How do you feel when you make a mistake?
- What is preventing you from forgiving others and yourself?

ACCEPT THAT YOU CAN MAKE MISTAKES. UNDERSTAND THAT SINCE YOU MADE IT THROUGH HERE, YOU ARE ALREADY A WINNER. LET GOD LOVE YOU THE WAY YOU ARE SO YOU CAN ALSO LOVE OTHERS THE WAY THEY ARE.

"...And forgive us our debts, as we forgive our debtors."
Matthew 6:11-12

Day 3:

YOU ARE MORE THAN ENOUGH

When you feel overwhelmed, exhausted, and suffocated, remember that less is more!

It's in the simplicity of things that you will find inspiration—the beauty of a flower, the sound of the rain, a walk in the park, or wearing a plain white shirt. We tend to accumulate unnecessary things, that doesn't matter in our lives. We become guarded, locked, closed, hidden, and cluttered.

Clean your closet and fix your drawers at home and at your office. By doing this, you will make space for something new in your life to occur. Let's be honest. Why do we need that many pairs of pants and shirts?

What about going paperless on bills? Less paper is more trees!

> **"LESS TIME MAKING CHOICES IS MORE TIME ENJOYING LIFE"**

The same thing goes for the heart. We wait for something new to happen, something new to flourish, but seldom do we make space for it, him, or her because we are holding on to the useless things of the past and toxic relationships.

FACING REGRET

A heart full of regrets can only produce condemnation and total blame on life's situations. Make space for a new beginning by letting go of the past and allow God to heal you.

And he said unto me, My grace is sufficient for thee: for my strength is made perfect in weakness.
II Corinthians 12:9a

No regret brings about no condemnation. No doubt yields more freedom, happiness, and strength. When you look back at your life through the eyes of grace, you will be able to accept your loss and even identify some lessons learned from each loss. There are some situations that are very difficult, but if you are willing to let go, God will take the lead and heal you.

Sometimes, we choose to hold on to those hurtful memories, and they become the perfect excuse for our resentful behavior toward life. We welcome the attention we receive when people sympathizes with us.

Unfortunately, we end up feeling as if we are never going to be good enough because of our past hurts and grief. That is why the apostle Paul teaches us to move forward and forget what's in the past by looking forward to what lies in the future.

Don't be afraid to unclutter your heart by forgiving so that you can embrace a new opportunity and forget the pain. Remember, you are more than enough for God because He is more than enough for you. He is always willing to embrace you.

※ How could you simplify your life right now on a daily basis?
※ What kind of thoughts about the past should you let go of?
※ How do you feel about giving yourself another chance?

UNCLUTTER

YOUR LIFE AND SOUL.

MAKE SPACE

FOR NEW THINGS,

AND

EXPECT GREATNESS

FROM

THE INSIDE OUT.

"He must increase; but I must decrease."
John 3:30

Day 4:

YOU ARE STRONG

Stop ignoring that you are running out of gas and refuel your tank.

Being caught up with a problem that could have been avoided is always frustrating. One day, I took my kids to the beach and instead of refueling the tank before hitting the road, I ignored the gas signal, thinking that I was going to find a gas station somewhere along the way but I was caught up with the wrong thoughts.

When I realized that the next gas stop was still far, I became very stressed. Instead of singing, laughing, and enjoying the trip with my kids, I was nervous and afraid that we would get stranded on the road should the car break down. I was begging God to help us not to get stuck on the road without gas. When I finally found a gas station, I almost let out a cry for I had put myself and my kids through an avoidable situation.

ALWAYS PAY ATTENTION TO THE SIGNS.

We must pay attention to our hearts as they signal what area requires specific care and support. Sometimes, we fear that facing those signals will only make it worst, but that is not true!

Unfortunately, just as we ignore the signal of the gas tank light in our car, we tend to ignore the signs of personal crises that could be prevented if put into consideration. A teenager should never ignore hormonal signs just as an executive should not ignore the signs of the stress.

A few years ago, I felt like giving up on everything because I looked around, and I couldn't find a reason to be happy. I felt as if I hadn't accomplished anything. I felt small, miserable, and unsuccessful. All I could see was hard work without rewards. I felt that I had exhausted my fuel long before my supposed destination. It was time for the "pit stop."

If you feel like I did, don't be afraid, and don't give up. Days as this creeps in to destabilize our faith but we must hold on. You are not going through a life crisis; you just need a life reset!

FACING FEAR

When you are fearful take a step back, slow yourself down a little bit, and take a good look at life from a different perspective. You will find that you have accomplished a lot and have many reasons to have hope.

You just need to make a "pit stop" to change your attitude and refuel in order to get back on the track just as they do at a car race.

I remember when I used to watch Formula One Racing with my father every Sunday. I used to feel bad when the driver had to stop to refuel and change tires.

Then one day, my father explained to me that a "pit stop" could be vital and help teams turn their race strategy from failure to success because with a new set of tires, the car will run faster which becomes an added advantage.

Also, during the stop, debris is removed from the radiator air intakes, and the car's windshield is cleaned up for better visibility.

A reset gives us an opportunity to remove the debris from our lives and the ability to clean the windshield of our hearts.

*Wherefore, seeing we also are compassed
about with so great a cloud of witnesses,
let us lay aside every weight, and sin which
so easily beset us. And let us run with patience
the race that is set before us.*
Hebrews 12:1

During different stages of our lives, we are constantly threatened by our insecurities, bombarded by a feeling that we are not capable and might never make it. Sometimes, the future seems unreachable, our strength begins to weaken, and we forget that God wants us to run the race and that He is our "pit stop." Hence, trust in Him to find refuge at all times. Because when we are weak, then we are strong because He is strong.

I will say of the Lord, "He is my refuge and my fortress, my God, in whom I trust." Psalm 91:2

You were created with the potential to execute your calling, so take a step back today, breathe, listen to your heart beat, count your blessings, and let hope rise within you. Reset it!

Dreamers don't go through midlife crises; they go through midlife resets!

※ What kind of signs have you been ignoring?

※ What are you going to do to bring about a change in your life?

※ What have you learned from your past mistakes?

> ***...whatsoever you do, do all to the glory of God.***
> I Corinthians 10:31b

LOOK AT
YOUR LOSSES AS A
LEARNING EXPERIENCE.
USE THE EXPERIENCE
AS FUEL
TO MAKE IT BETTER
NEXT TIME
EVEN IF YOU HAVE TO
TRY AGAIN AND AGAIN.

...in all these things, we are more than conquerors through him that loved us.
Romans 8:37

Day 5:

YOU ARE FLAWLESS

Is the glass half-full or half-empty?

How challenging it is to be able to look at things from a different angle! To be able to look at a loss with hope, for example. It is the ability to "read between the lines," and see things from an angle that includes what other people see as well.

> *"The light of the body is the eye:*
> *if therefore thine eye be single,*
> *thy whole body shall be full of light "*
> Mathew 6:22

We always want to perceive things in a way that we want, and it's usually in a way that we will certainly benefit from. But how about trying to look at a situation where you will actually benefit your neighbor, your husband, or your friend? Why do you always have to be right?

Respecting other people's perceptions helps us to avoid many conflicts. We don't have the power to change people, but through our actions, we can show them that their perceptions might not be accurate and this may influence their school of thought.

Since perception is the way we see things based on our experience, we need to constantly adjust the way we perceive life to avoid taking a negative approach that is based on our failures.

If failure becomes our starting point, sooner than expected, we will feel like our lives are a half-empty glass. But when we adjust our perception through the eyes of faith, our negative experiences will stop to influence our perception.

Stop looking at your life as a half-empty glass as if your marriage hasn't achieved its best moment or your dreams haven't even started to be fulfilled.

Instead, look at how far you have come, how much effort have you devoted, and you will see that you are already "half-way full." When we look at life with the eyes of faith, what appears to be half-empty will always become half-full.

> *"When we look at life with the eyes of faith,*
> *what appears to be half-empty*
> *will always become half-full."*

FACING PRIDE

I used to be a perfectionist, always striving to be the best in everything I did. I was always setting high-performance standards for my life, full of critical self-evaluations and extremely concerned about what others thought about me. I was always aiming to be flawless using my own strength to create a unique niche that would inspire lives around me.

I was very dedicated and competitive at work. I remember working as a teller at a banking center years ago, always achieving my goals and closing my cash box "to the penny," and never missing a cent. Until one day, I found myself missing $500 from my cash box. What a nightmare! I stayed almost two hours after the bank closed figuring out what may have happened and also tried to find it. I reviewed my transactions, and I counted my money over and over again. I did not want to accept my cash difference because that would mean accepting that I was wrong.

I kept thinking about what my peers would say. I did not want them to think that I was incompetent.

I was afraid to be criticized and have my reputation and my records ruined. Honestly, I was just full of pride, and I just had to overcome it.

The next day at work, I revised my process for coin exchange, and I perfected a few things that could have had caused that cash difference.

Through that mistake, I was able to revise my process and I eventually perfected it. That experience made me more aware of my process, and it never happened again.

Sometimes, being wrong is the right answer to a new discovery. It will give you an opportunity to learn something new, to apologize, to be vulnerable, and to show others that you are just yourself. Accepting that you are wrong can set you free from pride and save you from unseen distress.

> *"But I say unto you, That ye resist not evil: but whosoever shall smite thee on thy right cheek, turn to him the other also.*
> Matthew 5:39

Sometimes, we get so worried about making a good impression that we forget to be ourselves and connect with the right people. You don't need to formulate a perfect answer every time you are in a conversation. You don't need to know it all, and it shouldn't always be about you all the time!

A prideful person will always seek vengeance, but a humble one will be brave enough to turn the other cheek. When pride is eliminated, we become kind and compassionate, and give others the attention that they need.

For all have sinned, and come short of the glory of God; Being justified freely by his grace through the redemption that is in Christ Jesus.
Romans 3:23-24

We all have our flaws, and we all make mistakes every day. From losing our temper with our kid, being rude to a stranger, or telling a lie to the boss, we are just imperfect, and we need God's mercy every day we wake into a new dawn. Those attitudes are not examples of how God has called us to live, but we don't need to live in shame over our flaws. We need to be humble enough to surrender to God and become flawless through grace in Jesus Christ.

❋ How do you usually show God's love toward others?

❋ What could you improve to better your relationships?

❋ How do you feel about reshaping your thoughts about yourself?

EMBRACE A POSITIVE PERCEPTION IN LIFE WHILE SURRENDERING TO GOD'S GRACE.

For I know the thoughts that I think toward you, saith the Lord, thoughts of peace, and not of evil, to give you an expected end.
Jeremiah 29:11

Day 6:

YOU ARE AN INSPIRATION

What would your book title be all about?

We are always looking for something to inspire us to achieve our dreams and move forward in our lives. But often times, we forget that our lives are an inspiration to others as well. There are many people who are cheering for us because they have emulated out ways from a distance without our knowledge.

Nobody reads a book wishing it will be a disaster and a waste of time; people expect the best outcome. Your life is a book, and people can read you by simply looking at your expressions, your smile, and your posture. So, choose your book's cover and start living right by its title.

For as he thinketh in his heart, so is he:
Eat and drink, saith he to thee;
but his heart is not with thee.
Proverbs 23:7

If you believe you are an amazing mother, you will behave like one, and your kid's friends will wish they had a mother like you. If you think you are an amazing son, you will treat your mother so good that your mother's friends will wish they had you as their son.

Unfortunately, many people walk around feeling sorry for themselves, looking at life from an unfortunate perspective, and writing a book with a sad ending. Don't think that what you've been through was a fatality for no reason, but look back at those days and find within yourself that same strength that helped you overcome those difficult days. Stop putting yourself down and start believing in your ability to succeed.

FACING LOW SELF-ESTEEM

When our self-esteem is low, we hardly speak about dreams and plans. We become very suspicious about everything and overprotective about ourselves, and always afraid of being judged. Being able to dream during difficult times heals our soul while showing that we found a balance, an equilibrium, a goal that is bigger than the circumstances.

One of the best ways to overcome low self-esteem is by serving people the right way. It has been proven that people who volunteer feel more connected and have less conflicts. We often look for motivation in artists or celebrities, but how about getting motivated by serving the people in need? It unlocks gratefulness and exterminates selfishness inside of us.

For even the Son of man came not to be ministered unto, but to minister, and to give his life a ransom for many.
Mark 10:45

Sometimes, it is hard to serve when you are not appreciated or rewarded. Housewives often complain that their job is not recognized enough. When I left my job to dedicate more time to my teenagers, I felt the impact of working harder without a paycheck at the end of the week. At first, I felt so unworthy because I wasn't bringing the income anymore.

Then, I felt like I was doing the same job every day without any kind of visible improvement. There was always a pile of dirty dishes inside the sink somehow. Until the day that I understood what service was.

Jesus teaches us an amazing lesson about serving others when He washed the feet of His disciples. Think about it. If it was your last supper with your best friends, how would you want them to remember you? Maybe as the one who cracked the best jokes or the one who held it all together until the end? Jesus chose to be remembered as the one who washed everybody's dirty feet, teaching us about the highest position: being a servant.

Being a servant does not diminish your identity when you know who you truly are. When I learned that, it enabled me to serve in love. Cooking and cleaning became a privilege while washing the dishes became an opportunity to make my family happy.

> *Charity suffereth long, and is kind; charity envieth not; charity vaunteth not itself, is not puffed up, Doth not behave itself unseemly, seeketh not her own, is not easily provoked, thinketh no evil; Rejoiceth not in iniquity, but rejoiceth in the truth; Beareth all things, believeth all things, hopeth all things, endureth all things. Charity never faileth:*
> I Corinthians 13:4-8a

* How do you feel about being an inspiration to others?

* What kind of behaviors would you like to improve to feel good about yourself?

* What is preventing you from reinventing yourself?

SERVE YOUR FAMILY, YOUR FRIENDS, AND YOUR COWORKERS OUT OF LOVE INSTEAD OF OBLIGATION.

Wherefore comfort yourselves together, and edify one another, even as also ye do..
I Thessalonians 5:11

Day 7:

YOU ARE UNLIMITED

Dream the impossible dream. We can't afford not to.

When God took His people out of Egypt, He did not plan for them to stay in the desert for so long, but because they limited God with their thoughts and actions, the trip became a lifetime journey that took longer than expected.

> *Yea, they turned back and tempted God, and limited the Holy One of Israel.*
> Psalms 78:41

Unfortunately, we all tend to limit God with our small thinking.
Our circumstances should never define our thoughts. Instead, our thoughts should empower us to find solutions to our troubles.

> *Our mind is the place where we generate ideas, form conclusions, and build our visions.*

When our thinking process slows down, life passes by, opportunities are lost, and motivation by itself won't do the job.

We neglect priorities such as our spiritual life, and we spend a lot of time running after emergencies that were probably caused by procrastination.

When we feel overwhelmed, we sacrifice our time to dream, blocking our thinking and limiting God's action in our lives.

FACING PROCRASTINATION

We all struggle to find ways to get our schedules and our lives under control. Everybody is busy these days, and everybody knows that you are busy too. The whole world is moving faster and is expecting more of us at work, home, and everywhere else we go. We have a million excuses for feeling overwhelmed, for always being late, and for falling behind on our chores.

Accountability is one of the most important things to avoid procrastination. When you make yourself accountable, you become more responsible toward your priorities, and you stop waiting for God to do everything. When you take good care of your priorities, you eliminate most of your emergencies.

Redeeming the time, because the days are evil.
Ephesians 5:16

Just as we leave decisions and actions behind, so many times, we constantly leave God behind too.

When we are in tune with God as much as we should be, we become inspired by Him, and we start living under His standards. Innovation starts with inspiration.

It is time for you to increase your expectations, to shape your imagination, and to let God bring you into a new level of thoughts.

Knowing who you are in Christ is the key to courage, commitment, and actions.

Now unto him that is able to do exceeding abundantly above all that we ask or think, according to the power that worketh in us,
Ephesians 3:20

REMEMBER:
GOD IS INFINITE,
GOD IS ALMIGHTY,
GOD IS POWERFUL,
GOD IS JUST,
GOD IS IMMUTABLE,
GOD IS ETERNAL,
AND GOD CAN
DO EXCEEDINGLY
ABUNDANTLY
ABOVE ALL THAT
WE ASK.

"Stop trying to fit God into your small world and set time aside to let Him fit you into His unlimited world in order to enjoy several opportunities, because in God, you have infinite possibilities."

✸ What do you want to accomplish in the next five years?

✸ How often do you take time to dream? Why?

✸ What is limiting your vision?

DREAM THE IMPOSSIBLE, VALUE YOUR TIME, AND ADJUST YOUR DAILY SCHEDULE.

And be not conformed to this world: but be ye transformed by the renewing of your mind, that ye may prove what is that good, and acceptable, and perfect, will of God.
Romans 12:2

ABOUT THE AUTHOR

Adriana was born and raised in Curitiba Brazil. As a child, she had big dreams and a zeal to change the world. She didn't quite know it at the time, but her tenacity and adventurous spirit would lead her one day to the US where she would dedicate her life to serving God and helping others empower themselves to live full and purposely lives.

Having originally graduated with a degree in business, she began her career in Real estate and years later as an entrepreneur. After meeting her husband Eddie and having her two children Kevin and Kathlyn, Adriana took a reprieve from her professional life and decided to dedicate her time fully to raising her children. During these years, she experienced the love of motherhood, the challenges of womanhood and the necessity of resilience.

It was during this time or dedication, growth and reflection that Adriana realized her life's calling and began her service to her church and community at large.

Adriana later became a pastor for Home International Church as well as a counselor to her congregation and community. She began her coaching career with a certification in Life Coaching from the Life Coach Institute of Orange County in New York and is currently a Life Coach in private practice at Just Adriana, LLC.

Recently, inspired by her love and dedication to Christ and humanity, Adriana co-created the non-profit organization, Rice and Beans & H20 where she works to provide resources and spiritual guidance for the underprivileged communities of developing nations. In an effort to help others find themselves in Christ, Adriana has completed a mission trip to Haiti in 2017 and one to Ecuador in November 2018. She continues to seek the Lord daily for opportunities to help others find themselves.

CONTACT THE AUTHOR

Pastor Adriana Ferreira,
Certified Life Coach

www.justadriana.com

www.facebook.com/justadrianaferreira

Email: justadrianaferreira@gmail.com

www.instagram.com/just__adriana

God's Life
PUBLISHING

God's Life Publishing is a ministry of God's Life Christian Church, and is dedicated to making resources available to the Body of Christ in the form of printed publications and e-books.

All resources has been reviewed for its spiritual edification content before we publish them for the Body of Christ.

NEW JERSEY
744 Chancellor Ave
Irvington, New Jersey 07111
Phone: 973 986-5407

HAWAII
4998C E. Ehiku Way
Ewa Beach, Hawaii 96076
Phone: 973 986-5407

For distributor, dealers, store locations or ordering information:
call or send an email to:
godlife@aol.com

godslifepublishing.org